13.95

UNITED STATES SUPREME COURT LIBRARY

Anthony Kennedy

by Bob Italia

Published by Abdo & Daughters, 6535 Cecilia Circle, Edina, Minnesota 55439.

Copyright © 1992 by Abdo Consulting Group, Inc., Pentagon Tower, P.O. Box 36036, Minneapolis, Minnesota 55435. International copyrights reserved in all counties. No part of this book may be reproduced in any form without written permission from the publisher. Printed in the United States.

Photo credits: A/P Wide World Photos-cover, 4, 11, 24, 28
Archive Photos-17, 26
Globe Photos-14
UPI/Bettmann-7, 21, 23, 29, 30, 35

Edited by: Paul Deegan

Library of Congress Cataloging-in-Publication Data

Italia, Robert, 1955-
    Anthony Kennedy / written by Bob Italia ; [edited by Paul Deegan].
      p. cm. — (Supreme Court justices)
    Includes index.
    Summary: A career biography of Supreme Court Associate Justice Anthony Kennedy.
    ISBN 1-56239-094-5
    1. Kennedy, Anthony M., 1936-   —Juvenile literature. 2. Judges—United States—Biography—Juvenile literature. [1. Kennedy, Anthony M., 1936- . 2. Judges. 3. United States. Supreme Court—Biography.] I. Deegan, Paul J., 1937- . II. Title. III. Series.
KF8745.K46I86 1992
347.73'2634—dc20
[B]
[347.3073534]
[B]

                                                                    92-13710
                                                                       CIP
                                                                         AC

Table of Contents

Page	
5	Judging with Grace and Wisdom
6	The Son of a Gambler
9	"I Dare You to Get Arrested!"
10	A Restless Law Student in a Red Beetle
12	A Lawyer and a Lobbyist
15	A Political Career is Launched
19	Kennedy Joins the Supreme Court
27	Kennedy's Supreme Court Opinions
34	Burning the Flag
38	Outside the Court
39	Glossary
40	Index

Judging with Grace and Wisdom

Associate Justice Anthony Kennedy is a relative newcomer on the Supreme Court. Yet during his brief career on the Court, Kennedy has encountered some of the most politically charged issues of our time. He has responded by judging with grace and wisdom while upholding the Constitutional rights of Americans.

Anthony Kennedy with his family outside the Supreme Court building in Washington, D.C.

When the Senate approved Kennedy's nomination in 1988, political conservatives hoped his votes would consistently favor their positions. But Kennedy has defied the conservative label. He has become the moderate and balancing force that the Senate hoped he would be.

The Son of a Gambler

Anthony M. Kennedy was born in the depression year of 1936 in Sacramento, California. His mother, Gladys, was a school teacher. His father, Anthony J. Kennedy, was a politically active lawyer in California. The senior Kennedy, while a regular churchgoer, had a fondness for gambling. Anthony J. Kennedy paid his way through law school by winning poker games.

When Anthony M. Kennedy was nine years old, he got his first taste of California politics. Because Kennedy was very restless at school, his father got him a job as a page in the state senate in the hopes of controlling his son's nervous energy. There, Kennedy ran errands and messages for the legislators.

Backed up by family members, Judge Anthony Kennedy stands in front of the United States Supreme Court building. He was sworn in as the 104th U.S. Supreme Court Justice.

Young Kennedy developed an interest in politics while working as a page. He got to witness the excitement and intensity of all the floor debates. He saw legislators argue and battle each other while creating new state laws and deciding state budget matters. Also, his father would take Kennedy out of school to watch him present his cases in the courtroom.

"I probably saw ten jury trials before I was ever out of high school," said Kennedy. "I loved it."

"I Dare You to Get Arrested!"

Kennedy, a devout Roman Catholic, was an altar boy. He was also a good student and rarely got into trouble. This concerned his father. He worried that his son was becoming too straight.

One day, the elder Kennedy decided to do something about it. He offered his son $100 if he could somehow get arrested. But the straight-laced Kennedy couldn't manage the feat, and he never earned that $100 prize for being bad.

A Restless Law Student in a Red Beetle

When Kennedy was eighteen years old, he enrolled in Stanford University in Palo Alto, California. Kennedy majored in history and political science. He also studied constitutional law. There, Kennedy proved himself to be a brilliant student. He earned his college degree in just three years. Then he went to Europe and spent a year at the London School of Economics.

Private Kennedy (r) poses with his friend while serving in the National Guard in 1962 at Fort Ord, California.

While in Europe, Kennedy, still a restless young man, traveled extensively. For three months he toured the continent in a red Volkswagen Beetle. Once he had his fill of Europe, Kennedy returned to the United States and enrolled in the highly-regarded Harvard Law School in Cambridge, Massachusetts. In 1961, Kennedy graduated with a law degree.

A Lawyer and a Lobbyist

After graduation, Kennedy returned to California and took a legal job with a law firm in San Francisco. Then, in 1963, tragedy struck. Kennedy's father died, leaving no one to run his law firm.

Kennedy resigned his position in San Francisco and returned to Sacramento to take over his father's law firm. In addition to practicing law, Kennedy found that he also had to become a lobbyist for some of his new clients. That meant he had to meet with and entertain government officials on behalf of his clients. Two such clients were Schenley Industries, who sold liquor, and the California Association of Opticians.

Kennedy was a brilliant lawyer. His legal arguments were always well thought-out and well prepared. But he was not comfortable being a lobbyist.

Kennedy was more at home in the courtroom than in the halls and lobbies of the state legislature, where most lobbyists practiced their craft.

Said one of Kennedy's associates: "Tony Kennedy went more for the intellectual side of the law, instead of entertaining people."

A Political Career is Launched

That same year, Kennedy taught constitutional law class one night each week in nearby Stockton at the McGeorge School of Law in the University of the Pacific. He taught there for more than a decade.

In the early 1970s, Kennedy's work as a lobbyist and a teacher came to the attention of California Governor Ronald Reagan. Edwin Meese, Reagan's executive secretary, also took note of Kennedy's efforts.

Presidential secretary Edwin Meese took note of Kennedy's efforts.

Governor Reagan asked Kennedy to write Proposition One, a proposed law that would bring tax relief to the people of California. Proposition One was eventually defeated in the state legislature, but it gave birth to the famous Proposition thirteen, which ultimately granted the people of California an unheard of 50% cut in their property taxes.

Reagan was so pleased with Kennedy's effort that he recommended Kennedy for appointment to the Ninth Circuit Court of Appeals. President Ford took Reagan's recommendation and appointed Kennedy to the appelate court. The Senate confirmed Kennedy's appointment in 1975.

Anthony Kennedy spent thirteen years on the Ninth Circuit Court of Appeals. There he wrote more than 400 "opinions" (rulings) on decisions that were made by lesser courts. Sometimes these rulings "upheld" (agreed with) the lesser court's decisions. Sometimes these rulings "overturned" (reversed) the decisions.

Kennedy believed in the death penalty and life without parole.

While in the Circuit Court, Kennedy earned a reputation for thoroughness and fairness. Many times his rulings were considered conservative—but not always. That made it impossible to predict how he would rule.

When it came to some criminal matters, Judge Kennedy usually stayed in line with the conservatives. He believed in the death penalty and life imprisonment without parole.

Said Kennedy of these views: "An essential purpose of the criminal justice system is to provide a (means) by which a community expresses its collective outrage at the (aggression) of the criminal."

In one case, Kennedy allowed the admission of evidence even when the search warrant was considered invalid—as long as the evidence was seized "in good faith." This ruling was also considered a conservative view.

But in another case, Kennedy refused to allow the admission of evidence where the police bribed a five-year-old to tell them where his mother hid her drugs. In a clearly liberal tone, Kennedy declared: "I view the police practice here as both (destructive) in itself and dangerous as a precedent. Indifference to personal liberty is but the (forerunner) of the state's hostility to it."

Kennedy Joins the Supreme Court

In 1987, Associate Justice Lewis Powell decided to retire from the United States Supreme Court for health reasons. Powell, considered a moderate in his political views, had acted as a crucial balance between the conservative and liberal Court justices. Now there were fears among some senators that Ronald Reagan, now the President, would try to appoint an ultra-conservative justice. This would give the conservatives control of the Supreme Court.

While the Senate watched carefully, Reagan did indeed nominate a staunch conservative to take Lewis Powell's place on the Supreme Court. His name was Robert H. Bork. But before Bork could be confirmed, he had to be approved by the Senate.

Immediately, moderates and liberals worked hard to deny Bork a place on the Court.

Witnesses testified before the Senate Judiciary Committee that Bork was an ultraconservative (extremely conservative) who would become a rubber stamp of approval for President Reagan's conservative wishes. Issues such as abortion and rights for accused criminals—both of which Reagan opposed—were cited.

Pro-choice advocates rally to support the Roe vs. Wade decision in Denver, 1989.

Bork's ultraconservative views came out when he was questioned by the Judiciary Committee. Bork said he did not agree that the Constitution guaranteed U.S. citizens the right to privacy. Nor did he agree with a Supreme Court ruling in the 1960s that said married couples could practice birth control.

Bork's views disturbed many in the Senate. Bork's nomination was eventually defeated 58-42.

President Reagan and Attorney General Edwin Meese had to scramble to find someone else to appoint to the Court.

They decided that in order to receive Senate approval, the appointee had to be experienced both legally and politically. Nor could the appointee hold disturbing views like Robert Bork. Instantly, Anthony Kennedy's name came up. President Reagan quickly nominated him.

The Senate could find little fault with Anthony Kennedy. He was articulate, humble, and gracious throughout the confirmation hearings.

Judge Robert Bork (l) with President Ronald Reagan.

When asked about how his religious beliefs would influence his decision-making process, Kennedy replied: "It would be highly improper for a judge to allow his or her own personal or religious views to enter into a decision with respect to a constitutional matter."

And when asked how he would conduct himself as a Supreme Court Justice, Kennedy replied: "I am searching, as I think many judges are, for the correct balance in constitutional interpretation."

These moderate and intelligent responses brought sighs of relief from the Senate. By a vote of 97-0, Anthony Kennedy was approved by the Senate, and he officially became a Supreme Court Justice in 1988.

President Reagan (r) shakes hands with Judge Anthony Kennedy.

Kennedy's Supreme Court Opinions

It has been difficult to put a label on Justice Anthony Kennedy. Some think he is a libertarian. (A libertarian is someone opposed to government interference in people's lives.) Kennedy's rulings against unreasonable searches and seizures—like the case involving the bribed 5-year-old and his mother—seem to indicate a libertarian view.

But Kennedy has also shown that he is not interested in defending the rights of homosexuals, which is a conservative view. He upheld a lower court decision approving the dismissal of a homosexual from the Navy. He also upheld another lower court decision that approved the deportation of an Australian charged with homosexual activities.

Anthony Kennedy at the White House ceremony to become the 104th U.S. Supreme Court Justice.

Police arrest a protester after he set fire to the American flag on the steps of the Capitol building in 1989.

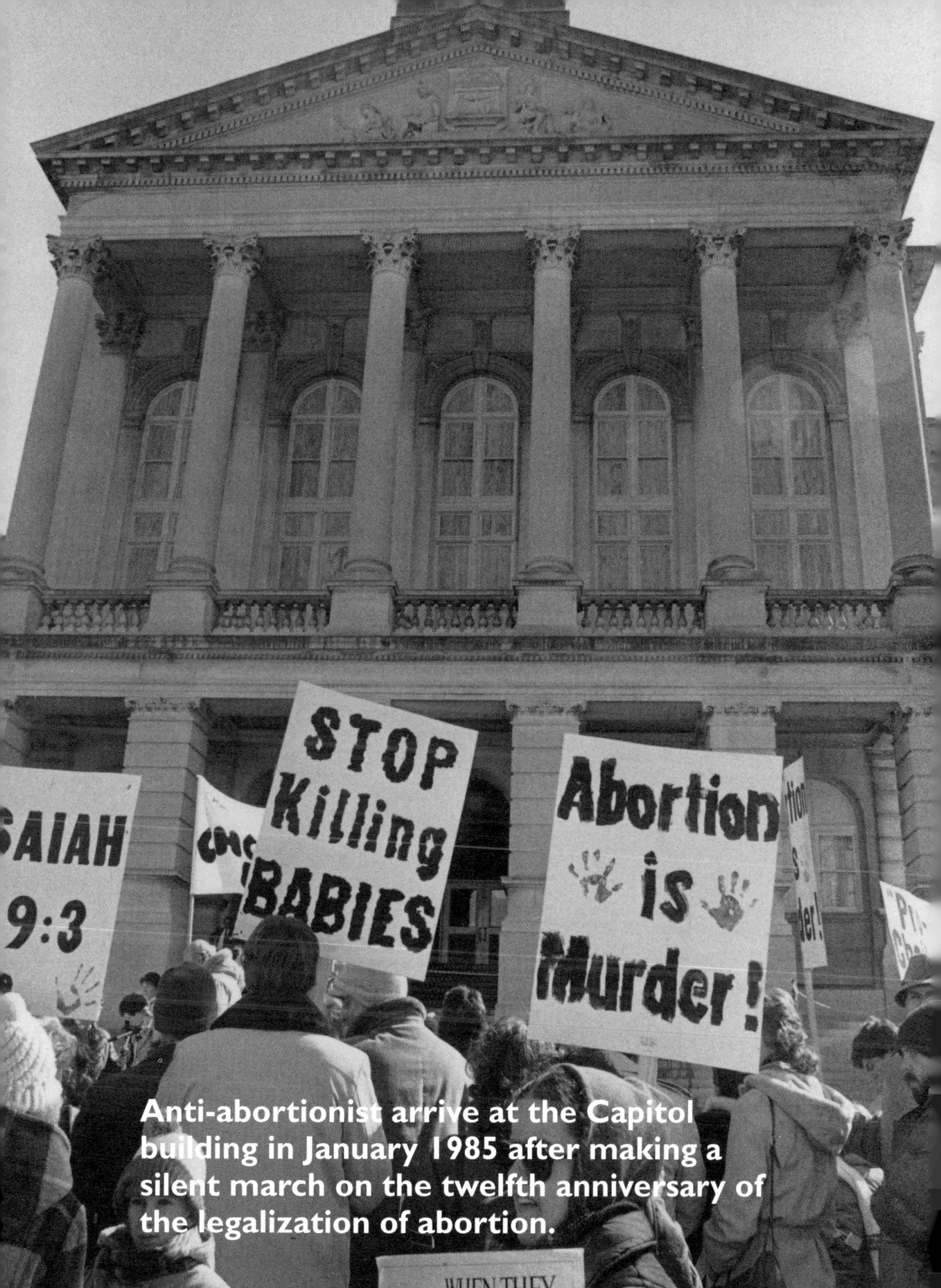

Anti-abortionist arrive at the Capitol building in January 1985 after making a silent march on the twelfth anniversary of the legalization of abortion.

Then again, there is Kennedy's defense of the rights to privacy—a libertarian viewpoint. Of these rights, Kennedy said: "It is central to the idea of the rule of law that there is a zone of liberty, where the individual can tell the government: Beyond this line you may not go."

In another ruling that disturbed conservatives everywhere, Kennedy defended a protester's right to burn the American flag. He has also refused to condemn the ruling that granted women the right to have an abortion.

When it comes to civil rights cases, involving race and sex discrimination, Anthony Kennedy is definitely conservative. Kennedy refused to condemn a real estate company when they were accused of steering white couples to white neighborhoods and black couples to black neighborhoods.

Supreme Court Chief Justice William Rehnquist.

And Kennedy voted to overturn a lower court decision that ruled against the state of Washington for paying male workers more money than female workers when both were doing the same kind of work. Kennedy has also voted consistently to make it more difficult to prove employment discrimination.

 Justice Kennedy remains loyal to conservative Chief Justice William Rehnquist when it comes to criminal cases. Kennedy has agreed that a 17-year-old could receive the death penalty for serious crimes. He also has agreed that police can destroy evidence before a criminal is brought to trial, unless the evidence is destroyed "in bad faith."

 When it comes to the issue of separation of church and state, Kennedy has been hard to figure. In one case involving the use of federal funds for church-run programs to promote chastity among teenagers, Kennedy agreed with Rehnquist and the majority of his fellow justices.

He felt this funding did not violate the First Amendment's requirement that matters of church and state remain separate.

But in another case involving the display of a Nativity scene inside a county courthouse, Kennedy did not agree with the majority of justices who said it was illegal. Kennedy felt that the First Amendment allowed local governments to celebrate holidays that had both a religious and secular (non-religious) theme.

Burning the Flag

By far, the most controversial case of Justice Kennedy's brief career has been the Flag Burning case.

In 1984, the Republican National Convention was taking place in Dallas. Gregory Johnson drenched an American flag with kerosene, then lit the flag on fire. Johnson was protesting President Reagan's policies.

People at the convention—and all across the country—were outraged. Johnson was arrested and charged with "desecration of a venerated object." The case made it all the way to the Supreme Court. Justice Kennedy's reply stunned the nation.

Gregory Johnson, whose conviction for burning a U.S. flag was overturned by the Supreme Court in 1989.

Justice Brennan wrote the majority opinion for the Court. The majority of justices ruled that Johnson's flag burning was a

symbolic act of freedom of speech guaranteed in the First Amendment of the Constitution. Therefore, the Court said that Johnson could not be charged with criminal activity. Nor could he be punished for it. Though he was not pleased with the ruling, Kennedy felt obligated by the Constitution to agree with the majority.

This decision further outraged people everywhere. The White House and some members of Congress called for a special Constitutional amendment that would protect the American flag. But after tempers had cooled and the ashes had settled, no amendment was approved. It was Anthony Kennedy's own words that best described why:

"I join this opinion without reservation, but with a keen sense that this case, like others before us from time to time, exacts its personal toll. The case before us illustrates better than most that the judicial power is often difficult to exercise. For we are presented with a clear and simple statute to be judged against a pure command of the Constitution.

"The hard fact is that sometimes we must make decisions that we do not like. We make them because they are right, right in the sense that the law and the Constitution, as we see them, compel the result. And so great is our commitment to the process that, except in the rare case, we do not pause to express distaste for the result, perhaps for fear of undermining a valued principle that dictates decision. This is one of those rare cases.

"For the record shows, this respondent was not a philosopher and perhaps did not even possess the ability to comprehend how repellent his statements must be to the Republic itself. But whether or not he could appreciate the enormity of the offense he gave, the fact remains that his acts were speech, in both the technical and the fundamental meaning of the Constitution. So I agree with the Court that he must go free."

Simply put, a Supreme Court Justice is a defender of our Constitutional rights. America can rest assured that Anthony Kennedy is doing the job he was appointed to do.

Outside the Court

Many of the Supreme Court Justices keep a low profile when it comes to their private lives. Justice Anthony Kennedy is no exception.

Kennedy lives with his wife, Mary, in a modest home in McLean, Virginia. Both share an interest in Shakespeare. In fact, Mary is on the board of trustees of the Folger Shakespeare Theater, located near the Supreme Court Building in Washington, D.C.

When he gets the chance, Kennedy likes to eat and jog with his law clerks at lunchtime. His favorite restaurant is called Hogs on the Hill, a barbecued ribs place near his office

Justice Anthony Kennedy is not a predictable justice. That is a good indication he will serve America well. He is at his best when dealing with the sensitive issue of free speech. Given time, Kennedy should prove to be one of the fairest and brightest legal minds of our time.

Glossary

Abortion: Expulsion of a human fetus during the first 12 weeks of gestation.

Conservative: Inclined to keep things as they are or were in the past.

Constitution: The fundamental law of a state which guides and limits the use of power by the government.

Controversy: A discussion marked by the expression of opposing views: Dispute.

Desecration: To violate something sacred, often in a way that provokes outrage.

Lobbyist: A group of persons engaged in representing a particular interest group.

Senate: A governing or lawmaking assembly. The Congress of the United States is the Senate and the House of Representatives.

Separation of Church and State: Constitutional guarantees preventing the government from endorsing religion.

United States Supreme Court: The highest court in the United States, which meets in Washington, D.C. It consists of eight associate justices and one chief justice.

Index

1st Amendment-32,33,34
Abortion-20,29,31
Birth control-20
Bork, Robert-19,20,22
Constitution-5,36,37
Death penalty-16,18
First Amendment-32,33,34
Kennedy, Anthony-5,6,8,9,12,13,15,16,18,22,
    25,27,31-34,36-38
Lobbyist-12
Meese, Edwin-15,20
Nativity scene-32
Proposition One-15
Proposition Thirteen-15
Reagan, Ronald-15,16,19,20,22,25,34
Rehnquist, William-31,32
Senate-5,16,19,22,25
Separation of Church and State-32
Supreme Court Justice-25,37,38
Supreme Court-5,19,22,25,34